Hidden Emotions

THE SPOKEN WORDS

OF MY DEEPEST FEELINGS

LAMAR SMITH

Hidden Emotions

THE SPOKEN WORDS

OF MY DEEPEST FEELINGS

Quisqueyana Press
Poway, California, USA
info@quisqueyanapress.com
www.quisqueyanapress.com

Table of content

INTRODUCTION

Experience my deepest emotions, the ones that hide from the general eyes, and are expressed as spoken words in the form of rhythmic and arrhythmic verses that create poetry. Know my secret feelings. The ones that are difficult to talk about. The ones with life on their own that one day make my heart race, brought me into tears and keep my mind busy, until I was able to let them be born as musical words that spoke for themselves, revealing my story, undressing my feelings, expressing my thought, bringing to these pages word by word my hidden emotions.

Journey through my book as I transform negative emotions into art, and paint fictional affairs that reveal the real me, the one who lives inside.

DEDICATION

I dedicate this book to my mother for showing me what true love and strength are. Second, I dedicate this book to my father for helping me understand what it means to love selflessly. Also, to Mousey and the rest of the Rockheads family for giving me the information needed to publish my first book. Last, this is to all of those who relate to my poems, hoping my words could help heal the pain afflicted upon your hearts.

Thank you!!!!!!

"You never know how strong you can be, until being strong is the only choice you have left."

-Tupac Shakur

She's Mine

"She's mine"!!!! is something I repeatedly told myself.

As I watched her come home from school

from across the street.

As I watched her smile at her mother, I imagined her smiling at me.

Looking at her light brown eyes,

glimmering like honey in the sunlight.

Her dark brown hair smoothly glided between her fingers.

Looking at me as she tilts her head in satisfaction.

As she enters her home, I eventually snapped out of it,

my heart racing in anticipation of that one day to finally ask her out.

At night, as I lay in bed,

all I can ever do is think about her saying hi to me,

While remembering how she sounds while greeting me.

Her voice is like heaven in the form of a sound.

It fills your soul with euphoria, along with many chills.

She's so gorgeous, I hope every time that one day she'll notice me

taking the long way home from school, hoping to run into her.

We're not together, but she's the charger to my battery,

the motivation behind the long walks I take after school.

Seeing her on my way home is like hitting the mega millions jackpot.

It's rare to see her but yet it's not impossible.

For now, I will continue feeling satisfaction from seeing her come

home from my doorstep,

because every day I experience the best part of the day,

and that's looking at her smile while reflecting on how "she's mine"

07/22/2021

A Quiet Encounter

As I rode the train, I sat across from the most beautiful girl,

whose hair was dark brown, and long with many curls.

She had eyes that were blue, and they sparkled like the sea.

She knew she had my attention when she finally looked at me.

I was forced to hold my gaze.

I couldn't resist the strength of her eyes.

Her stare said a thousand words,

It reminded me of a morning sky.

The train was fully crowded,

with many focused on their phones

but as the girl and I locked eyes,

It was as if we were all alone.

My heart began to race, and butterflies filled my stomach.

I heard the conductor's voice saying the next stop was coming.

I began working up the courage to introduce myself,

but the fear on the inside interfered with how I felt.

When my stop came, I looked away and walked off the train

I thought to myself, "I should've at least told her my name."

I walked on the two platforms looking at the uniquely shaped tile,

then turned around as the train rode off

and the girl left me with a smile.

Today, I invariably think about it,

it's something I can't let go of...

I may have ruined a shot with my soulmate

because of my fear of love.

04/11/2019 - 05/03/2019

A Resident at Heart

S ighing...
so full of despair,

as I hopelessly put old memories into this box.

My heart was so pure for her,

but her heart was as hard as volcanic rocks.

Once upon a time, I lived within the abundance of her heart.

Rent-free.

So warm and spacious, so grateful.

Living in a home I wasn't sharing,

it was only me, but I was startled one time

when I came upon new boxes in my home.

They weren't mine; they were foreign.

I'm supposed to be here alone.

So much anger began to build as the boxes multiplied over time.

My home has begun to thump to a new beat.

I took that as a sign.

Full of mixed emotions because these new items here aren't mine.

I no longer feel comfortable in my home

and things are feeling wicked.

So much changed in a place I call home.

I realize I'm getting evicted.

For so long, I was tormented, day and night, with anxiety.

I feel resistance in this place so often that I feel that it's fighting me.

Finally, I saw one box had the name David.

It all made sense; these are the answers that I had lonely awaited.

Without saying a word, I left.

Because the rhythm of these beats is no longer for me.

There's nothing I can do anymore.

I'm just happy that I can see.

Now, as I put these memories in this box,

I'm thinking about how to transition from "we" to "I".

But the hardest part is guessing about how to move on without

saying goodbye.

07/22/2021

A Friendship I'll Never Forget

There was a 70 year age gap between two friends.

Both were experiencing a pain

that only a friendship could mend.

This friendship caught me by surprise.

I couldn't comprehend,

it's funny how life works with the people God would send.

He was my favorite resident at Cortland Park nursing home.

He was brimming with positivity, but he constantly felt alone.

He always made my night with a funny joke or two.

We laughed until we cried,

he told me "I always have fun with you."

He experienced pain all day and night.

and slept peacefully,

but when he opened his eyes, he had to fight.

Every day, he fought with that level of pain and agony.

But one thing I admired was that he still kept his hospitality.

He was a genuine friend... in fact, one I'll never forget.

I guess every sunrise will always have to set.

01/06/2020

A Poem about Love

I always stayed to myself in my own world of Independence
and minding my business.

Never truly experienced love,

but it was something I always witnessed.

Two people merging together,

to make one beautiful life.

First boyfriend and girlfriend,

second engagement, then husband and wife.

Love can be weird with two opposites

falling because of Cupid.

Yet it's so strong,

making someone like Albert Einstein stupid.

It's something I don't understand,

yet it sparks my curiosity.

Like why girls desire good men,

but date guys who lack generosity.

See, I really don't understand.

But do I desire love? Maybe!!!

I Just have a habit of quietly dismissing myself

when someone seems shady.

I'm not sure, I'm indecisive.

But I've been thinking about it lately.

Maybe I should do me

and wait for God to connect me to the right lady.

05/08/2021

Alone in Solitude

When I'm alone, I sit in solitude on my own.

Thinking about my past and how much I've really grown.

The silence is addicting that's why I'm frequently "low key".

It always keeps me humble cause I'm with the "real me".

In silence, I think about all my flaws,

my strengths and weaknesses.

Taking time from those

who suck and drain my energy like leaches.

Some people would call me fake,

because I'm very distant.

Not knowing I'm very observant,

I see things and become resistant.

But I understand I may turn people off

with my aloofness,

staying to myself, not saying enough,

and leaving people clueless.

To many, it may appear immature,

but to me, solitude is like healing,

recharging my emotional battery

and healing from things I've been feeling.

It's not on purpose.

Being laid back is part of my personality.

I'll never neglect time alone in solitude

because I have a better sense of reality.

09/28/2018

Art

Before I draw, I observe the image of my inspiration.
Processing every detail, taking my mind away like a vacation.

Searching for the areas that look easy or where I may struggle.

Thinking about what if, and how I can make that mistake very

subtle?

Then I search for the specific tools needed for the piece.

Looking for the right color like a lion who's ready to feast,

then I begin to make gentle strokes along with the sheet

In a room of solitude, quiet enough to hear my heartbeat.

Where I begin an open dialogue between me and myself.

Saying I like this!!!

No, let me erase the ears. He sort of resembles an elf.

Then I'll begin to shade, coloring until I can feel.

Feeling all the negative emotions leave until I've begun to heal.

Expressing my emotions using my artistic desire.

Finishing my masterpiece with a heart ignited by fire.

My brain releases hormones, so many endorphins I feel higher.

And then, I finish successfully drawing a piece that'll one day inspire.

11/22/20

Brilliance

S o bright!!
It is when it shines.

It's light from above, brimming with its angelic illumination.

Its strength and warmth provide when it's at its highest.

Darkness dashing in fear of its overpowering luminosity.

But the drastic changes that are in effect as it descends,

sluggishly descending while darkness slowly prevails.

Darkness comes out of hiding as the fire weakens.

Concealing all land in a temporary dark coat,

the air's quality falls into a cool, cold breeze.

Dark, cold, and quiet as space provides light.

But a change drastically takes place as the little light descends.

Creatures come out of hiding, aware of the occurrence.

Startled, as darkness slowly retreats.

An orange haze appears as the light slowly progress,

peeking above the horizon,

while slowly conquering the unilluminated,

ascending triumphantly as it returns with its luminosity.

Air quality rises as it returns with its warmth.

Once again, so bright!!! It is when it shines from above.

Brimming with its angelic illumination,

Its strength and warmth provide at their highest.

While it sheds comfort, warmth, and light on a nation.

04/25/2021

Bloomed

From the day you were a seed,
you laid right in the palm of my hand.

You were so small to the naked eye,

like that of a grain of sand,

when I placed it in the soil,

you laid right before my eyes.

How small you were, camouflaging to the point that I did not realize.

As I watered you for 5 days, I watched to see your progress.

I was so ecstatic, mixed with the anticipation to witness your process.

But I guess because I was watching you, I didn't see any growth.

It's like the more I overlooked you, the more you grew the most.

I noticed how beautiful you were

growing with a sweet sense and of great posture.

So tall and erect to the point

that I thought for a sec that you were an imposter.

You started to grow when I paid less attention,

as if you knew I wasn't watching.

I watered you every day,

but it's as if you pretended to experience a thirst

that was parching.

I still love how much you've grown,

though there was so much I did not see

you bloomed into a beautiful flower with a fresh scent

that still to this day satisfies me.

09/19/21

Drink

It's hot, scorching heat,
with no sign of a cool breeze.

Fatigued from exhaustion,

while continuously sweating out my white tees.

So parched, so dehydrated, and desiring a nice cold drink.

Desiring a cold beverage so much that I can barely think.

An ice-cold drink is what I seek,

quenching and ending my undying thirst.

I saw my drink on the table, but before I took a sip,

I admired how mouthwatering it looked first.

Watching as the condensation drips down

as if it were trying to tease me.

As I took a step closer to grab it,

I can feel a sense of peace, as if the effects of thirst released me.

I realized that even before taking a sip,

I no longer felt uneasy

It's as if this tormenting feeling of thirst

knew I was about to drink and chose to leave me.

I know it sounds crazy, but believe me.

I guess the sight of finally seeing an ice-cold drink relieved me.

As I drank, I felt a cold sensation,

a feeling that immediately pleased me.

I never thought about that

while feeling deeply parched,

the sight of an ice-cold drink would intrigue me.

07/24/21

Different

Y es, I do have feelings on the inside.

They're just hard for me to express.

Music, poetry, and solitude

are my way of escaping the ongoing stress.

Sometimes I reply and say the wrong things,

but I have good intentions, or sometimes I may remain silent.

Then, later on, think of things I should've mentioned.

No, I'm not upset, nor are they're people I hate.

I just hate that people assume they're correct

thinking I'm angry and that's a mistake.

I understand I am different,

I'm independent and handle things on my own.

At the same time, it's not bad asking for help.

This plays a major role in how much I've grown.

I don't show my deepest feelings much,

but when I love, I promise I love deeply.

I express this love with those I trust

by communicating freely.

I love the way I am.

I'm more in tune with my emotions.

Poetry made this possible

because it gave me a voice when I was broken.

I didn't choose this way to express myself.

It chose me, so I guess I'm chosen.

Why?

'cus on the outside, I look street

but inside my heart is truly golden.

So, time alone is therapeutic.

It's all that I need

for when I feel slow and overwhelmed,

solitude has always got me back in speed.

I know I am different.

A better word for it is unique.

Someone who understands me is something

I'll forever seek.

04/22/21

Healing

She's beautiful and in love.

but yet she's so scared

because she was taken for granted

with how much she really cared.

She loves him a lot, but yet she's really hurt,

because her ex saw girls and always wanted to flirt.

She shuts down because she fears the future

regardless of how she feels, part of her is scared he might use her.

She's angry because she wanted to be better.

part of her sees herself with him together.

She didn't plan on falling in love.

It kinda caught her off guard.

She always tried to retreat out of fear,

but it was hard.

So unpredictable love is,

with no clue of approaching

Catching her off guard in the process of hoping.

Hoping to one day find a guy who truly loves her.

Imagining a guy who,

no matter what terms they're on, would hug her.

She's healing. She knows if he treats her wrong,

she'll start peeling, reversing her process,

and eventually returning those old feelings:

the anger, the fear, the depression.

She learned from her old relationship.

She already took that lesson.

She needs to be loved differently from other girls.

She needs patience and protection,

like clams protecting pearls.

07/22/21

Fully Guarded

F orgive me for being so guarded,
placing distance between us.

Though we get along so well,

I'm still struggling with trust.

See, my past is full of broken promises

and unmet expectations.

This caused me to become toxic,

making those I love sign applications.

Feeling them out to prevent myself from getting hurt,

reminding myself nonstop that I need to be aware,

that I need to stay alert.

Oh, how overwhelming it is guarding my heart

and preparing for a false reality.

I'll rather fall back to keep from hurting others with my

inconsistency.

It's part of my morality.

I'm sorry for allowing my issues to keep a gap

between the connection we have.

Spending more time catching up once in a blue

instead of sharing a daily laugh.

It hurts to know that I'm the one

who continuously makes and breaks your heart.

But trust me, it may hurt that I'm gone.

But this space between us will give you a fresh start.

09/18/21

Her Last Blessing

S he sat down, feeling hopeless and full of despair
and used her smile as a mask that she would every so often wear.

She felt like no one understood the sorrow she felt inside

so, she thought it was better to swallow her feelings and hide.

She already had five children, she didn't think she'll have another,

reliving that same process of once again becoming a mother.

While pregnant with her 6th child, she battled with depression,

only to find out that same year that her baby was a blessing.

While raising her last child; she decided to keep her head up.

She put a smile on her face `cus she knew she couldn't let up.

Regardless of her past, she remained an exceptional mother

Loving all her children with a love like no other.

She became both parents, and she did it on her own.

She's the definition of strength with the example that she's shown.

The amount of love she demonstrates, I can't get it from another

I'm grateful to be her son and to call her my mother.

10/18/18

Hidden Emotions

Feeling....as a young man in society,
this word means that I'm a punk.

Being labeled as a soft sensitive sissy

for not throwing my feelings away like it's junk.

For genuinely confessing and accepting how I feel,

instead of having so much pride.

It takes strength to openly express certain feelings

when you're tempted to hide.

Society says it's normal.

The average man must be strong all the time,

Twenty-four seven.

But there are grown men smiling, living life daily,

but died emotionally at the age of eleven.

See, I understand that this right here plays a role

because I struggle with anger,

bottling and suppressing so many past emotions

until it eventually led me to danger.

But I'm done...... I'm tired of obeying and trying to look cool

for people who don't care about me as God does.

Because God forbid if I ever reacted out of anger

in response to silly situations,

they won't hesitate to say, "And he's always angry too."

Society forces us, men, to not show emotion,

but when we get angry, we're the bad guys.

Telling our children to get up

and be a man and men don't cry...

We must stop these wicked lies.

I thank God for introducing me

to the art of spoken word poetry,

because it's through words where I can
relax....breath... express
and continue to take in the wisdom in which life is showing me.

09/19/21

I Love You... Pop

I love you...

Before, it was hard to say these three words.

Because of the anger and resentment that were overflowing my heart and my mind, up countless nights anxiously thinking, "What can I do to grasp your attention this time?"

Angrily wept because of the amount of stress that occurred for trying to gain dominance in a situation I had no control of.

Crying while punching my pillows violently, while shouting: why? And what I do?

Reminiscing, trying to capture my earliest memories when you were home but instead, I cry.... because I barely remember you.

How foolish.... I used to go without contacting you for so long, thinking that you would at least think about me and reach out, but I was wrong.

Though you weren't there, my mother had extra help and did everything she could to raise me. Raising me with a broken heart and being extra strong for her last baby.

See, now I'm grown, but looking back, you never made it on one occasion. I remember `cus my mother and Anthony Holloway were the only two who made it to my kindergarten graduation.

You were a no-show at my fifth-grade graduation and behind closed doors, my heart was tearing. Again, this time, the only two who made it there were my mother and my older brother, Darren.
I also made it through 8th grade, I promise,
that graduation I'll never forget.

I was popular; I had good grades, and I played the drums at my ceremony, missing that I know you'll definitely regret. But by the

time I made it to high school, I was struggling with depression, from years of being angry deep down in my heart and continuously stressing.

I was so genuinely tired, mentally and emotionally.
It was so bad that I couldn't express myself openly.

My attendances in high school were terrible, all I ever wanted to do was to stay home. I was angry, stressed, and tired. I just wanted to stay in my room alone. I went through it because I wanted your attention. I genuinely wanted you.

How could you make memories with me when my brain was barely developed at the age of two? Playing with baby Lamar, making him laugh, but today I don't have one clue.

See, though my attendance in high school was poor...

...yo pop, I still made it.

I walked across that stage in my cap and gown, but you still didn't

show up; I hate it.

See, it's not you who I hate, it's just the fact that you're still the same.

See, every time I graduated, I got a congratulation, starting with

Lamar and ending with your last name: Smith.......

It's crazy how you barely showed or did anything for me.

But yet I respect you.

`Cus, now that I think about it,

you probably never had a father yourself,

or at least someone to correct you.

I never thought I would actually be saying this, but pop,

I understand you.

I understand the struggle of growing up without a dad

and trying to become a man.

But stan...... I have to let you go; I have to release you from my mind,

my heart, and my soul, or I won't grow.

It's not easy and I've been trying for the longest too.

But I'm proud of myself `cus at the age of twenty-one I can finally

say

... I love you

04/25/2021

Insecure

S he's so ashamed of her weight

because she isn't shaped like a model.

She has so many insecurities

to the point that she can write a novel.

She's ashamed of her stretch marks

because they would affect the appearance of her skin.

Wishing she never gained weight

and imagining she was thin.

She's so ashamed of her laugh,

thinking that it sounds so goofy.

So, she tried to control and change it

because it didn't match her beauty.

She's so ashamed of her appearance,

she's not happy with her body.

So, she dresses to hide her shape

because the appearance of herself is foggy.

She's ashamed of her face

because she thinks she isn't beautiful.

Comparing herself to another woman

is what she does daily.

To her, it is the usual.

She's insecure about her age,

sometimes reminiscing about being young.

Not liking her shape and appearance,

or sometimes wishing she had more fun.

She doesn't like how tall she is,

always overthinking about her height.

Most guys are more attracted to short girls with heels

because more height is what they like.

See, there's beauty in stretch marks

because they tell a story.

Whether she had a baby, lost or gained weight,

it's still congratulatory.

There's beauty in all women,

no matter the size, weight, or appearance.

There're beautiful models of different sizes,

don't let opinions make a mental interference.

The sound of our voice is unique

whether talking or laughing.

Sometimes our goofy laugh makes jokes funnier

to the point, you might find some people tapping.

All women are uniquely beautiful

because there's only one version of you.

So, love yourself and enjoy this life

because we only have one chance to live it, not two.

09/20/21

Love

L ove... it means loving someone who's perfectly imperfect,
choosing one person to go through thick and thin with

because they're worth it.

One person to occupy your heart for a lifetime,

leaving it unavailable to many.

Someone who, regardless of what they go through,

stress, hurt, pain, love for you, they still have plenty.

Valuably caring for you with a love that's different from others.

A type of love we haven't recognized

since being raised by our mothers.

Each other's heartbeat synchronized,

beating to the same song.

And no matter the issue, struggle, or circumstance,

love will always get along.

08/04/21

Loving through darkness

How can a person see in the dark?
Pitch black darkness without a match to spark.
This darkness brings fear, terror, and anxiety,
maybe this darkness has a purpose.
Maybe I was blinded to see.
Maybe the darkness is a test, an obstacle, or maybe a challenge,
fighting me as I struggle to use positive thoughts as a balance.

This darkness can represent any situation we face in this life.
To cut, stab, and break us like the sharp end of a knife.
Only the strong can survive with the power of love,
whether it's family, friends, or God
cornering you with the wings of a dove.

Darkness can sometimes be present in the company of love,
hiding in plain sight like that of a hand inside of a glove.
Much may speak of the struggle of loving through darkness.
Trying to love while there is this thing
that's trying or causing you to become heartless.

See, love conquers all sins, fear, basically anything
This is the truth, so if you're giving up,
this means you've been let go of many things
Just hold on, no matter how bad or strong the darkness is.

I know the feeling of the anger and frustration
bubbling up like Pepsi's fizz,
but remember, loving through tough times is special
'cus it causes the weak to love less,
but the few strong people who endure,
takes on the challenge and gives it their best.

04/22/21

Midnight

I always used to see you appear above the night sky.

Choosing to come out at sundown,

I wondered if you were shy.

Gently providing light at the deepest hour of the night.

When I see all of you fully, it's the most beautiful sight.

You show up in many shapes and forms,

yet you continue to glow.

Sometimes clouds would try to block you,

but your light continues to show.

I remember seeing you glow red.

I wondered who made you angry.

I figured it was the sun during daylight savings,

taking so long and it made you cranky.

I wanted to fly high through the sky,

just to get a closer view

because it's rare to see you in red.

It happens once in a blue.

You are so thoughtful,

when you appear, you bring the stars too.

I just wanted to show my appreciation because,

sadly, many forget to notice you.

07/24/21

A Paradox

I'm living in a paradox,
the more I move forward,

the more I want to step back,

desiring to step back

regardless of if I'm on the right track.

As I move closer to my destiny,

I slowly grow in fear.

An uncomfortable feeling of uneasiness

that I can no longer bear.

As I move closer to my destiny,

I'm seeing my desires change.

Fewer people, no desire to box.

This new version of me is strange.

My life is the true definition of the word paradoxology,

causing me to look at life from two different angles,

like I'm in geometry.

I also notice, the higher you rise,

the lower you must go.

As you are being elevated,

humbleness should naturally flow.

I don't understand life

because things are drastically changing.

Maybe I just need to trust God

`cus it might be him rearranging.

05/04 - 05/05/2019

Love From the Outside

As I stand outside the house,
gazing at the yellow-lit windows.

I feel joy, peace, and love

as the window slowly covers with snow.

Standing here

watching my family gather in unity.

To be able to witness my family together

is such a great opportunity.

The amount of love I see here

is genuinely like no other.

All I see is laughter and smiles

as my siblings hug each other.

Though I hear holiday music

playing in the background.

Love is the only thing I hear,

overpowering every sound.

It's amazing being in there

and talking amongst my family.

But as I stand here emotionally broken,

it's the only thing keeping my sanity.

07/24/21

Misinterpretation of my Kindness

I was once angry,
overflowing with so much resentment and emotion.

Consuming myself with rage,

drowning in negativity like an ocean.

I was foolishly lashing out,

releasing this anger with violence.

People think I'm crazy,

or something is wrong as they watch in silence.

While some looked at me with a sense of delight,

they were pleased and proud.

While, on the other hand,

I was feeling guilt

with a conscience that was loud,

desiring to change,

do to of my reputation of anger and poor decisions.

What a struggle it is to hear God with a temper

continuously fighting me to listen.

I finally changed at some point,

thanks to the help I received through Jesus Christ.

Molding me to mature,

becoming more loving, respectful and nice.

So calm, cool, and collected, and yet,

still, I am provoked.

It's as if me changing for the better,

to some is only a joke.

People thinking because I'm calm,

they can use me and take my kindness for weakness.

People think they're more superior

because I practice meekness.

I'm not arrogant, Instead,

I'm humbled before God as well as people.

There's not one person who's better than another.

God made us all equal.

I refuse to change back

due to the mindset and actions of people.

`Cus, in actuality, they're the ones

who avoid self-reflection `cus they're see-through,

but last, I know better.

I'm avoiding conviction by the high.

I wanna be ready for any moves he makes.

I don't have time for him passing me by.

Those out there who provoke me,

I know a lot of them wouldn't see this.

That's why I distance myself from those

who takes my kindness for weakness......

09/20/21

My Best Friend

I wanna be better, but this time I'm ready.
Trust me, I'm not that 16 years old

who sat there and allowed their emotions to become heavy.

See, when I briefly look back in the past,

I see I had so many friends,

and now I'm looking at my life,

now, and all I see is so many ends.

But there's still one last friend that still remains,

who stayed through all the failures, mistakes,

and even through all the shame.

And yet to think how terribly I treated him throughout the past,

continuously be inconsistent and ignoring his task.

I'm known as a fighter,

but I'm removing that mask.

I no longer desire to fight my battles,

please take this `cus I pass.

I'm letting go of the old me, slowly but truly,

with faith and hoping you'll (one day) use me.

To show you how much I truly care,

if I had one trillion dollars to spend,

I'll give it away, just to consistently be your friend.

You remained by my side through the darkness,

even during those moments,

where I may have been perceived as heartless.

You are being so loving and giving your life for mine,

just so you can give me a chance

to stand up, stand out, and shine.

I don't fully understand your love (for sinners)

you came to die, you rose, and you freed us.

I can go on about how amazing you are, but instead,

I'll conclude with their words, ... Thank you, Jesus.

04/21/21

This is Who We Are

I'm a young child of God
living in a world that listens to society,

which says we must do wrong to fit in.

Do I really want this world defying me?

In this world, unholy things are normal,

such as gangs, fights, and drug use.

But when we mention true love in Chris Jesus,

many fall back with a big excuse.

Do we really want to be a part

of a world that rejects the son of man?

Who persecutes and hates us,

just for being apart from God's plan?

The world celebrates those in prison,

rather than those who are new in Christ

and respects those with hard hearts

that are as cold as arctic ice.

But as followers of the most high

we must remain in this light,

So, we can be an example to the world while

looking good in God's sight.

See, this is who we are, strong disciples of Jesus Christ.

Followers of the one who rose from the grave

and victoriously freed us.

He is our heavenly father,

who, in the beginning, loved us first.

This is why I'm proud to be a child of God

and friends with the creator of the universe.

03/29/19

My Queen

She continued to smile but on the inside,
she was low.

I don't know anyone like her.

She's the strongest queen I know.

While going through, she loved me

`cus she knew I was the last.

She continued to raise me despite her past.

She's my Queen

I remember all the nights when she would sing,

sing songs about spring,

I'm thankful for the joy she used to bring,

at times, while I'm thinking, I would usually reminisce,

thinking about the old days, those times I'll forever miss.

Ma' this poem is for you,

This poem you truly inspired.

Because of your strength while raising me,

waking me up for school while you were mentally tired.

Those moments when you wanted to cry

but saw me laughing, so you started smiling.

Give me your last bite of food

while your stomach was growling.

You are the reason I have such respect for women,

respecting yourself and telling me off

when I was as sour as a lemon.

I can't ever pay you back.

While raising me, you were so strong.

Thank you, mama, for putting me first,

and keeping your head up for so long.

09/30/18

EDITOR NOTES:
In the book editing process, we do not alter the contractions and slang words contain in the poems in honor of respecting the poet's style.

Visit my author page at
www.QuisqueyanaPress.com/Lamar-Smith

If you enjoy this book, please don't forget to live a review on Amazon,
this will be greatly appreciated.

CPSIA information can be obtained
at www.ICGtesting.com
Printed in the USA
BVHW041001270122
627130BV00023B/2396